If I Were President

Compiled by Peggy Gavan
Illustrated by Janice Kinnealy

Troll Associates

CHAPTER 1

✶ What would *you* do if you were elected President of the United States?

That's the question we asked kids across America as part of our *If I Were President* contest. And the mail came pouring in! Thousands of "future presidential candidates" sent us their ideas on topics like the national debt, unemployment, poverty, the environment, and life at the White House.

The very best ideas — imaginative, innovative, and humorous — were compiled and put into this book. Each student's name and grade appear next to their response. (When we received duplicate responses, we chose the earliest entry.) At the back of the book, you'll find an alphabetical list of winners, along with their schools and school addresses.

Finally, we would like to thank all the students who entered the contest and the teachers who encouraged them.

Living at the White House

I would paint the White House blue! I would have a green bedroom, a pet elephant, and a giraffe!
(Dale Kitchenmaster, Grade 2)

I would put baseball diamonds on the White House lawn. I would have the World Series held there. I would be assured of a great seat.
(Christopher Werger, Grade 5)

I would let my friends live with me in the White House if they didn't bother me when I was working.
(Christine Ecker, Grade 3)

I would let people visit the White House and see me.
(Jonathan Heathcock, Grade 5)

Everybody would get a special day to meet me and ask me an important question when I have free time.
(Aaron Kurup, Grade 3)

I would build a pizza parlor by the White House so I could eat pizza every day.
(Devon Blenkush, Grade 5)

I would buy a pool and put it in the backyard, fill it with soda, and swim in it all day.
(Kevin Drace, Grade 7)

I would be happy forever. I would take care of my gold and I would have a big bookshelf. The shelf would be very, very big. I would read 100 pages a day. And I would get married to a man. I would have three dogs, four cats, and five kids. I would help the poor and I would give the poor some of my gold.
(Leila Hamedih, Grade 3)

I would take all the animals in shelters and put them in the White House until I could find a good home for them.
(Jillian Weeks, Grade 6)

"Give Me Your Tired, Your Poor..."

I would find a way to help the poor people in our country. I would do this by sending special groups of people out to all poor people to make sure they have clothes and food. And the most important thing of all is to make sure they have a home or shelter, because no one should have to live in the street.

(Brooke Weber, Grade 3)

I would help the poor by not allowing restaurants to throw away leftover food. They would have to give it to the poor.

(Spencer Daigle, Grade 2)

I would have myself and members of the Congress live like the people in the working class to see and to understand what is going on in the United States.

(Michael A. Sutton, Grade 5)

I would open a government supermarket for poor people where healthy food would be sold for extremely low prices.
(Amy Willis, Grade 5)

There would be no more poor people because I'd make it rain money.
(Allison Marlune, Kindergarten)

I would build new homes for the poor and get doctors for them. And then I would give each and every one of them $700.
(Aaron Belk, Grade 3)

Peanut Butter

I would stop the wasting of food. I would give it to the poor.

(Marlo LaMonte, Grade 1)

I would have a drive for poor people in every state. Whoever would want to help would give a minimum amount of one dollar a day for three months to help the poor people in their state.

(Katy Law, Grade 6)

I would help the poor people find jobs and give them sandwiches.

(Justin McMurray, Grade 3)

I would give the hungry people food, the poor people money, and the sick people in the hospital toys.
(*Cody Daniel, Grade 2*)

I would lower the price of houses so people without much money could buy them.
(*Aaron Vincent, Grade 2*)

A Healthy America

I have had a pacemaker since I was four years old. My mommy says I am lucky because I had good doctors, and she says that not all kids have a chance to see good doctors when they are sick. So if I were president, I would make sure that all children and adults could see a good doctor.

(Lindsey Dewald, Grade 4)

I would do something about medical care, because many people get sick and die. I would get some volunteer doctors and they would serve for free one time a week. I would try very hard to make a medicine for AIDS.

(Stuart Abram, Grade 3)

I would give poor people free health checkups.

(Matthew DeGeeter, Grade 2)

I would help people with mental and physical disabilities, because there are so many children and adults with physical and mental disorders. These people need special care and attention. So to help these people, I would build special hospitals and invest money in medical cures. By building these hospitals and investing in cures, people would be able to get the care and treatment they need, and they would be around people with similar disorders, so they wouldn't feel isolated.

(Amy Burk, Grade 8)

I would give more money for AIDS research and other diseases such as cancer. I would make equal health insurance for everyone.

(Joei McKinley, Grade 5)

I would spend more money on research for rare disorders, such as Tourettes Syndrome. I would do this because I have this disorder, and no one understands it.

(Amber Pierce, Grade 8)

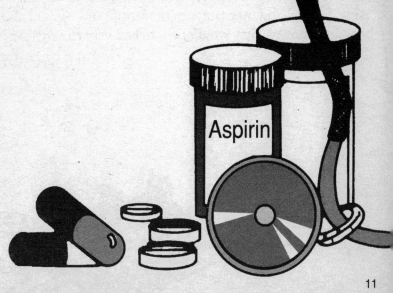

Protecting Nature

I would tell the presidents of other countries to stop destroying the rain forests. I would tell them to stop cutting down the trees, because if you cut all the trees down, one day you might need that plant and it will be all gone.

(Collette Plaisance, Grade 2)

I would not let people use animals for experiments, and would stop people from killing animals' habitats. I would protect animals' rights.

(Caraleigh Buxie, Grade 5)

I would make a law to prevent people from cutting down forests and trees. The only way one could cut down some trees would be with a special permit from me. I would assign certain rangers and police or volunteers to watch over forests and areas with many trees. If anyone got caught cutting down trees they would be fined an amount of money depending on how many trees they cut down. Their name, license, and other important identification would also be written down. They would be watched very closely from then on.

(Lori Beth Petruzzi, Grade 5)

I would help save the rain forests because there are important plants in rain forests that could save lives. I'd tell the people who are cutting down the rain forests to sell the medicines from the plants to make their money, rather than destroying the trees. After all, lumber will rot, but medicine will save lives. Trees are our main source of oxygen, so we need to conserve them.

(Mary Ramsower, Grade 4)

I would stop the killing of endangered animals. When animals are killed, it almost makes me cry. So many people kill animals just for fur coats, and I don't like that.

(Alia Short, Grade 3)

I would make laws about keeping the Earth clean and I wouldn't let anyone hunt whales. Also, no one would be able to hunt endangered animals or pick endangered plants. If someone cut down a tree, they would have to plant three new ones.

(Jenny Dubridge, Grade 4)

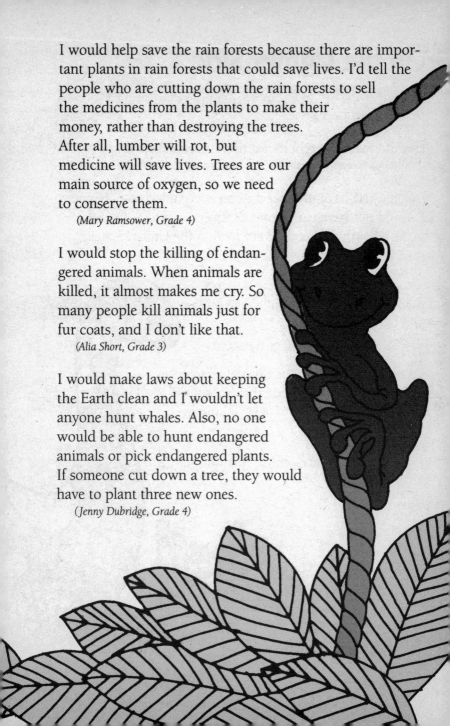

On the Lighter Side

I would stock up on a four-year supply of aspirin.
(Kristin Spell, Grade 6)

I would make everybody eat their green vegetables.
(Rebecca Blasenheim, Grade 1)

I would not have my speeches on every television channel.
I would not have car payments. Every Saturday, I would
make everything free at every mall in the United States.
And I would want my face on the $500 bill.
(Vincent Venegas, Grade 4)

I would love people — like give hugs
and kisses on the nose.
(Heather Mehall, Kindergarten)

I'd let everybody see the dinosaurs again,
and I'd let everybody ride the dinosaurs.
And I'd let everybody get everything free.
(Anthony Ritz, Grade 3)

I would put my face on Mt. Rushmore.
(Billy Fletcher, Grade 3)

I'm President!

I would always talk in a deep voice to let everyone know I was serious. I would not go fishing every day.

(Gabriel George, Grade 8)

I would be so happy that I would pop and explode. I would laugh so hard I would lose my voice. I'd be screaming, "Mom, I'm president!"

(Lena Lopez, Grade 3)

I would have Polka dancing every Saturday. People would be so busy dancing, they would not be able to have drugs and alcohol! I could also stop the gangs. I would catch them and talk to them, and tell them they have to read to the homeless. I would tell them they could go Polka dancing every day.

(Caroline Van Lanen, Grade 2)

I would probably be late for my own inauguration.

(Tom Cornell, Grade 6)

I would lower the price on Ferraris to $4,000.
(Stacy Phillips, Grade 3)

I would thank the people for picking me!
(Tisha Cline, Grade 3)

I would have pizza delivered to every-one's house on Friday nights.
(Christy Passeri, Grade 1)

I would write my life story. I would advertise it at the end of every speech. I would say, "Not many people know my life story. Now you can. Just buy this book. Only $198.99 for paperback and $199.99 hardcover." I don't think I would sell many books.
(Michael Sunshine, Grade 4)

I would lower the money my mama pays on bills.
(Kornetta Brown, Grade 1)

Educating America

I would first make it possible to receive a good education, which is the right of all people. I would make colleges affordable to all people who are qualified. I would do this by making grants and scholarships easier to get. Loans would be easier to pay back, and they would have no interest.

(*Justin Mitulinski, Grade 6*)

I would try to visit every school to talk about what I do every day, and let students visit the White House.

(*Monica Gonzalez, Grade 5*)

I would have free public college education.

(*Contessa Smith, Grade 3*)

Instead of spending money on private airplanes, helicopters, and limousines, I would spend it on children's education.

(*Andrew Bartell, Grade 4*)

I would want kids to study hard and do the best they could do. I would help them do this by giving $1 for every "A" on their report card. This dollar would be put into the bank and could be only used for college.
(Rebecca Nelson, Grade 3)

If kids drop out of school, I would take their driver's license away. How? I'd ask them nicely.
(Ryan Ehresman, Grade 2)

I would tell all the teachers to give more and more homework to children so they would learn more and more.
(Susan Watson, Grade 2)

I would make every school open in the summer so kids who don't have a place to go in the summer could still go to school. They would be summer school camps.
(John D'Alterio, Grade 5)

I would try to make school a little longer because people aren't getting enough education to make it in the world today. People need a better education.
(Sean Hilliard, Grade 8)

I would let students pay off college loans with community service.

(Sarah Sandherr, Grade 7)

I would pay more to the teachers for our education and give more money to schools for their supplies.

(Sandie Galan, Grade 5)

I would make a plan to send people without a high school diploma back for a year of schooling and vocational school. If they passed, they would be given their diploma, and they would be given a job as soon as possible. In my plan, anyone with a high school diploma or general equivalency diploma will be guaranteed a job, and extra money for bills and medical expenses.

(Trina Archer, Grade 6)

I would make year-round school because children forget things they were taught during school over the summer. With school all year round, kids won't forget things and teachers can start teaching them new things at the beginning of each year.

(Astria Naylor, Grade 4)

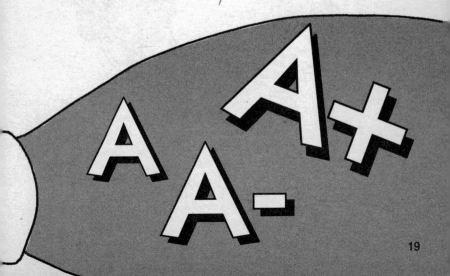

Working in America

Some people can't afford child care at all, so they just stay home. But if I were president, the government and/or big companies could pay for child care in the work place, and then people could work and earn money. There would be more people paying taxes, so it would all even out.

(Corrie Anderson, Grade 6)

For people starting their own businesses, I would lower their taxes for 10 years. If they are successful for 8 of those years, I would put them back on regular taxes.

(Lucas Rountree, Grade 4)

The first thing I would do is stop lending money to other countries who do not pay back the debt. I would then use that money to create more jobs for people. If there are not enough jobs for less-skilled workers, I would put them through training.

(Nicole Vallejo, Grade 8)

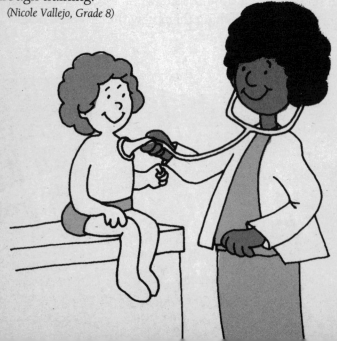

I would stop foreign countries from bringing their products into our country unless they let us bring our products into their country.

(Dianna Anderson, Grade 7)

I would trade things rather than use money. For instance, say a doctor goes into a grocery store. He wants to buy some food, but he doesn't have enough money to buy all the food he wants. He could tell the store owner, "If you give me this food, I'll give you a free appointment at my office." They could trade.

(Jeralynn Joy Beaird, Grade 5)

I would let women do all the things that men do, and make sure they get paid the same. There shouldn't be certain jobs for men, and certain jobs for women.

(Natalie Bonaretti, Grade 5)

Many people have lost their jobs and need to be retrained so they can find new jobs. If I were president, I would give a tax break to businesses that were willing to hire and retrain these workers.

(Stephanie Watts, Grade 8)

A Chance For Peace

I would stop spending so much money for weapons. The money I saved would be divided into three parts. The first part would be spent to build homes for the homeless and new schools, with computer terminals, for each student in all the cities of the United States. The second part would be spent for research to find a cure for major illnesses, such as cancer, AIDS, and Muscular Dystrophy. There would be money for families to pay for doctor care and hospital care if they are needed. The third part would be spent to develop new businesses which would create new jobs for many of the unemployed.
  (Elisa Melchiori, Grade 6)

I would take all the weapons and throw them in the sea. The Army would use squirt guns and water balloons to fight the wars.
  (Matt Morris, Grade 4)

I would declare another national holiday, probably around June 16. My holiday would be National Peace Day. I would hope no crimes would be committed on this day. Also, if a war was going on, a truce would be called in observance of this day.
  (Misti Moseley, Grade 7)

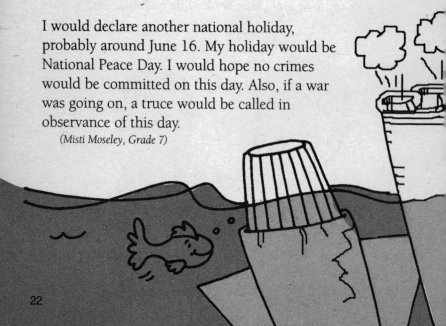

I would stop the fighting by telling everyone, "Please stop fighting," and I would stop the wars.

(*Peter Nekos, Grade 1*)

I would ask the members of the United Nations to sign an agreement to destroy all of their countries' missiles and bombs. Then if that worked, I would ask the United Nations to sign a peace treaty that said there would be no more wars between nations, and there would be eternal peace.

(*Don Lassus, Grade 5*)

Instead of wasting money on weapons when we're not even having a war, I would use it for school supplies.

(*Matthew Lang, Grade 4*)

If there was a problem between two countries, I would put the leaders of those countries together in one room and let *them* argue it out!

(*Erica Sanieoff, Grade 4*)

I would cut back on nuclear warheads because we have enough nuclear warheads to blow up the entire earth many times. Then I would give the money we would be saving on weapons to get our schools ready for the 21st century.

(*Amy Ackerman, Grade 8*)

I would outlaw the privilege to buy guns. Guns are dangerous weapons. Guns are like a representative of war. If war is wrong so are guns. We do not need guns in our country.

(*Courtney Lawler, Grade 5*)

I would do the best I could to make an effort with other super-power countries to destroy the nuclear weapons.

(*Damien Heffern, Grade 9*)

There will be no wars. I will make (leaders) sit in a room and not let them out until they are friends.

(*Kate Rosenfeld, Grade 3*)

I would make a law stating that when a person who has children buys a gun, they must be given a free strongbox large enough for the gun and bullets to fit in, and a good lock to lock the box. I would do that so the children do not get killed, and hopefully, not even hurt.

(*Crystal Lynn Griffith, Grade 5*)

Peace and Love

Helping the Homeless

I wouldn't spend so much money on things such as huge inauguration parties and large, formal dinners. I would spend the extra money on things we need such as food and shelter for the homeless.

(Ruth Bartholomew, Grade 7)

I would put up a shelter in every state — maybe two in the big states. These shelters would be almost like apartments. Each apartment could fit approximately four people, and there would be about 40 apartments in one building. Each family would get an apartment with two bedrooms, living room, and a kitchen. There would be a food store with donated food, and another room where the people could get donated clothes. I really think this would work out if everybody chipped in a little.

(Stacy Simek, Grade 5)

I would let all the homeless people live with me and let them be happy.

(Belen Torres, Grade 5)

for Everyone

I would take all the dogs and cats off the streets and give them good homes, and stop putting them to sleep unless the animal is suffering.

(Meghann Judd, Grade 3)

I would get construction workers to rebuild burnt-out houses and repair them for homeless people to live in. Then I would educate the homeless people so they can get jobs and support their families better.

(Thomas Fricano, Grade 3)

I would fix the problem of the homeless by sending letters to soldiers asking them to go where there are homeless people. Then the soldiers would help them build houses to live in.

(Ashley Brotherton, Grade 3)

I would give at least half of the money from state lottery tickets to the homeless to help buy food, clothing, and shelter.

(Kamielle Unruh, Grade 5)

One program I would greatly consider would be a "Room for the Homeless" program. People who have an extra room in their house and let a registered homeless person move in would receive a reasonable tax cut. The homeless person(s) must be registered with a county or state social service program and be clear of any criminal record. This would enable the homeless person to have a place to bathe and an address to list on his or her job resume. This system could also apply to an apartment owner who sets aside an apartment or two for homeless people.

(Christopher Schulman, Grade 6)

I would solve the homeless problem by making log cabins out of logs and mud. I would create jobs by paying people to plant trees and clean the land.

(Jeff Sparks, Grade 6)

I would give everyone a home for $10.

(Derrick Krakau, Grade 5)

Balancing the Budget

I would try to help solve the biggest problem facing America: the rising and bloated deficit. I would work for a balanced budget amendment to the Constitution so that my generation and my children's generation will not have to pay for the poor government we've had in the past few decades.

(Lauren Halliday, Grade 6)

I would try to cut the pay in the White House, the House of Representatives, and the Senate, and put that money toward the deficit problem.

(Veronica Phillips, Grade 5)

I would like to ask all the people of the United States to donate at least $1 all at once so we could apply it to the national debt.

(Amy Hecker, Grade 5)

I would raise taxes. I would do this because it is the only way I can foresee reducing the national debt. In addition to raising taxes, I would also make large cuts in our nation's budget. The items that would "get the ax" would be aid to foreign countries, as well as our nation's defense budget. I know that my ideas will probably be unpopular with a lot of people, but I believe that it must be done to save our great nation.

(Mark Tapazian, Grade 8)

I would make a law stating that members of Congress can't vote for their own pay raises.

(Nik Larsen, Grade 6)

I would rent out Camp David as a resort during the summer months and use the profits to pay off the national debt.

(Lisa Zeller, Grade 8)

Keep America Beautiful

I would do something about the environment. People talk about homelessness, poverty, and the economy, but none of that will matter if we don't have a safe and clean environment to live in. If we don't take the proper precautions, then there won't even be a safe and clean world for the coming generations.

(Lisanne Chatfield, Grade 8)

I would stop people who litter. I don't want people littering because it's bad for plants, animals, and birds.

(Stacey Johnson, Grade 2)

I would try to inhabit another planet so we could start over again, and not ruin our new planet this time.

(Laurie Simmons, Grade 6)

The first thing I would do is have a big parade, so that I could meet all the people. I would tell them that we have to make America more beautiful. From now on, anyone caught littering would have to work at the dump for one week with no pay. Everyone who recycles would get one free day off from work. I would have a contest to see which state is the cleanest. The winner would be our capital for the year.

(Adriana Cimino, Grade 2)

I would have a day every month when everyone would get out of school and off from work to clean the earth and make it a better place to live.

(Mike Katzman, Grade 7)

I would sew up the tremendous hole in the ozone layer.
(*Kari Culver, Grade 4*)

There would be more astronauts so they could go to
Mercury and the Moon. They could check to see if we could
live there. Then this planet wouldn't be so crowded!
(*Emily Mills, Grade 5*)

I would look for other kinds of energy, such as solar power,
windmills, water mills, and other discoveries made by
science. I would tell everyone not to waste water, electricity,
or food, and most of all, not to be a litterbug.
(*Kaitlin O'Donnell, Grade 4*)

I'd make the world a better place to be. I'd try to help the environment. I'd put up "No Littering" signs everywhere. I'd build a huge wildlife museum and give the animals good care. I'd try to make people recycle more, too.

(David Evans, Grade 4)

I would make new cars that don't use gas. These cars would burn grass clippings.

(Timothy Omlor, Grade 1)

I would make big businesses clean up and protect the environment.

(Shawn Baneck, Grade 3)

The War on Drugs

I wouldn't let big people give little people drugs.
  (Jeffrey Collins, Grade 1)

I would take the money that the police officers get from the drug arrests and give 25 percent to the police department that makes the arrest to buy new equipment to make more arrests. The rest of the money would go toward the very high national debt to start raising the economy. My reason for this is to reward the police departments fairly, lower the national debt, help the economy, and help get drugs out of America.
  (Kathryn Stickell, Grade 7)

I would get rid of all drugs by gathering all the drugs that I can, putting them into a rocket, and sending it to Mars.
  (Marques Hall, Grade 5)

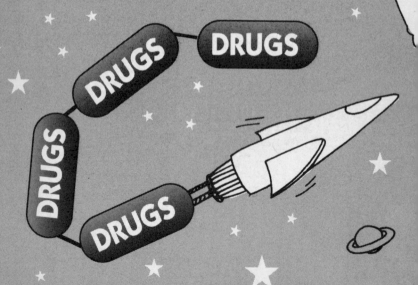

I would demand that each and every school in the U.S. have a drug and alcohol awareness class at least once a week. If you don't teach children about drugs, they won't know how harmful they really are.

(Allison Davies, Grade 5)

I would make sure the only drugs we would have would be medicines.

(John Rowleau, Grade 3)

I would put drugs in a big machine that flattens them and makes them disappear.

(Josh Lindeman, Grade 4)

To control drugs and alcohol, I will put special machines in cars, and if they smell drugs or alcohol, the cars won't start.

(Aaron Miller, Grade 4)

Around the Town

 I would make sure we have police on every corner to keep people from breaking the law, and so nobody gets hurt. I would also make sure we have plenty of parks for children to play in so they don't hang out in busy streets and get hit by cars.

(Brandon S. Authement, Grade 4)

There would be no more toll machines when you go over a bridge.

(Caridad Cortes, Grade 5)

I would put up more traffic lights so there wouldn't be so many car accidents.

(Mandy Sugimoto, Grade 4)

I will make sure that wearing seat belts is a mandatory law in every state. Also, all seat belts in all cars would have to pass tests to make sure they are safe. Only when they are safe may those cars roll out of the dealerships.

(Colleen Danaher, Grade 6)

If I were president and I could choose a good thing, it would be to build more libraries, because reading is peaceful and safe.

(Rachel Stork, Grade 4)

I would not let there be any more big traffic.

(Stephen Fohl, Grade 2)

For the People

I would try to please the people of this country. I would work mostly on health care, education, drug abuse, and the economy. I would definitely not lie about anything. I would always do what I promised, and I would do it right. Many people count on the president of the United States. Therefore, I believe he or she should be truthful and hard-working.

(Brooke Gill, Grade 7)

I would let everybody go on vacation — that would be the life! And I would feed the poor and let the poor people go on vacation for free.

(Sarah Johnson, Grade 2)

I would relate to the people. Instead of keeping things "top secret," I would tell the people. Even if I did wrong I would admit it and try to correct it. The key to making a country work is to be true to the people.

(Mary McAllister, Grade 8)

I would think about Abraham Lincoln and George Washington, and what they did to make our country great. We should unite the white and the black, and people of all

cultures. Democrats and Republicans should unite also. We should all come together and think of the best ways to solve the economic problems of our country. I believe that when we are able to come together, and stop fighting amongst ourselves, we will get along a lot better.

(Caroline Chesnutt, Grade 6)

I would try to end racism by ticketing anyone who is discriminating against another human being. If they still choose to discriminate, their tickets will be doubled, and so on.

(Nikki Cook, Grade 5)

I would lower the ticket prices to get into events or fun activities because many people don't get to see the neat things that go on in the United States.

(Tyler Lainson, Grade 7)

I would do more things for women's rights. I would let them have the same salary that men get, so they can support themselves better. I would also give women more opportunities for government positions. That way women would have more power in our nation and it would be equal.

(Arshia Quader, Grade 8)

I would make more national holidays. There would be a National Parent Day, a day for children to give presents of appreciation to their moms and dads. There would be a National Hamburger Day, and everyone would eat hamburgers for supper. I would also make a National Animal Day, when all animals get a treat of some kind.

(Katy Piatt, Grade 6)

I would give out lots of free kisses to everyone I met.

(Nida Hallal, Kindergarten)

I would make the homes for the elderly more cheerful and happy, because the elderly people were the lawyers and teachers and moms and dads who made this world what it is today.

(Moniqa Lopez, Grade 4)

I would save the people from dying. I would save the animals from dying. I would save the turtles from dying. I would save fish from dying. I would save my mom and dad from dying.

(Kate Gilchrist, Grade 1)

I would make handicapped people and people in nursing homes smile.

(Tom Mezzanotte, Grade 3)

I would add another day to the week called Funday. On Funday there would be no school, no work, and no chores. And every Funday would be considered a holiday, so people everywhere would have to do something fun on Funday.

(Hollie Harvey, Grade 6)

I think it would be important to put up opinion boxes for voters. I would put them in courthouses, post offices, and public libraries in each city. By having these boxes, I would know what the people in each city are expecting from me as their president. The people would also be better informed of what the president was doing for our country.

(Misty Crisp, Grade 4)

I would let women be able to do everything men can do. I don't think it is fair that there has never been a woman president. I think we need to change that.

(Sara Brotherton, Grade 7)

I would like to make people nicer and kinder to each other, and not kill each other.

(John Douglas Irvin III, Grade 1)

Ms. President!

For Kids Only

I would declare June 25 Kids' Day. For that one day, kids would run the government. They could start new bills and laws, and they could start petitions. Every government official would choose a kid to take their job for one day. Children could write essays, letters, and reports on why they wanted that government job, and they would study and take a test on the American government. I think this would be a good way to get kids interested in and involved in the government.

(Miray Samaan, Grade 6)

I would make the parents raise the allowances for kids.

(Samantha Roberts, Grade 3)

I would be sort of famous because I would be the first woman president. I would travel on a private plane. The Secret Service men will follow me wherever I go to make sure I'm safe. My main concern would be the children, and to make sure they had things to eat.

(Tiffany Peterson, Grade 4)

I would adopt all the children in orphanages.

(Michael D. Cranwell Jr., Grade 3)

I would make more exercise play-grounds. I think kids need more exercise to stay healthy.

(Nathan Burkholder, Grade 3)

I would make a news show for kids with a children's vocabulary and make additional speeches just for kids! I would gladly listen to the president's speeches if I could understand them! So if I were president, I would make an additional speech just for kids.

(Natalie M. Burg, Grade 5)

I would make more youth centers available, because youths are turning to drugs and violence. Youths are the future adults of our country, and we need to give them somewhere to go and someone to turn to.

(Elizabeth O'Brien, Grade 7)

I would focus on the problem of child care. Many parents try to teach their children what to do when they are home alone, but still many children are hurt or killed by fires or other accidents because they do not have the proper training to deal with emergency situations. I think this problem could be improved if child care was available to everyone, regardless of income.

(Rikki Hullinger, Grade 7)

I would lower the voting age to 15. I think teens are mature enough to make wise decisions by then. I would also raise the drinking age to 25. No store keeper in his right mind would mistake a teenager for a 25-year-old.

(Jennifer Franks, Grade 6)

I would give homes to kids. I would give kids candy. I would give kids food. I would put kids in school to learn. I would give kids parents. I would give kids books. I would give kids gifts so they won't feel lonely, but so they will feel good.

(Sarah LaPointe, Grade 2)

I would shrink all the grown-ups.

(Kaleigh Huddy, Grade 2)

I would visit sick kids in the hospital that needed a laugh. I'm sure they would get a kick out of seeing the president of the United States of America.

(Thomas Owens, Grade 6)

I would suggest a four-day school week. I would let the kids work in the community on Fridays. There are many ways they could work. They could clean the community or help people with special needs. And on Fridays after work they would get paid with gumdrops for a reward.

(Nicole Dittoe, Grade 2)

I would listen to what children have to say about our government. After all, they will be tomorrow's leaders.

(Danah Maertz, Grade 7)

A Special Thanks To:

- Abram, Stuart, Grade 3, Littlebrook School, Princeton, NJ
- Ackerman, Amy, Grade 8, Bryant E. Moore School, Ellsworth, ME
- Anderson, Corrie, Grade 6, St. Michael's School, Duluth, MN
- Anderson, Dianna, Grade 7, Carrithers Middle School, Louisville, KY
- Archer, Trina, Grade 6, Clinton Elementary School, Clinton, TX
- Authement, Brandon S., Grade 4, Davis Elementary School, Austin, TX
- Baneck, Shawn, Grade 3, Marathon Elementary School, Marathon, WI
- Bartell, Andrew, Grade 4, Shirley Kohls-Wilson School, Beaver Dam, WI
- Bartholomew, Ruth, Grade 7, Riverview Middle School, Barron, WI
- Beaird, Jeralynn Joy, Grade 5, First Baptist Lakewood, Long Beach, CA
- Belk, Aaron, Grade 3, Alma Intermediate School, Alma, AR
- Blasenheim, Rebecca, Grade 1, Children's Connection Day School, Baldwin, NY
- Blenkush, Devon, Grade 5, Concow School, Oroville CA
- Bonaretti, Natalie, Grade 5, Our Lady of Mt. Carmel School, Kenosha, WI
- Brotherton, Ashley, Grade 3, Rock Springs School, Denver, NC
- Brotherton, Sara, Grade 7, Huntsville Middle School, Huntsville, AL
- Brown, Kornetta, Grade 1, Pope Elementary School, Jackson, TN
- Burg, Natalie M., Grade 5, Tawas City Elementary School, Tawas City, MI
- Burk, Amy, Grade 8, Casey Junior High School, Mt. Vernon, IL
- Burkholder, Nathan, Grade 3, Plains Elementary School, Timberville, VA
- Buxie, Caraleigh, Grade 5, Hidden Forest Elementary School, San Antonio, TX
- Chatfield, Lisanne, Grade 8, St. Justin School, Santa Clara, CA
- Chesnutt, Caroline, Grade 6, Renner Middle School, Plano, TX
- Cimino, Adriana, Grade 2, A.C. Whelan School, Revere, MA
- Cline, Tisha, Grade 3, Sam Houston Elementary School, Ennis, TX
- Collins, Jeffrey, Grade 1, Cheshire Elementary School, Cheshire, MA
- Cook, Nikki, Grade 5, Lincoln School, Hartford, WI
- Cornell, Tom, Grade 6 , John W. Turner Elementary School, Chautauqua, NY
- Cortes, Caridad, Grade 5, St. Benedict Joseph Labre School, Richmond Hill, NY
- Cranwell, Michael D. Jr., Grade 3, Herman L. Horn Elementary School, Vinton, VA
- Crisp, Misty, Grade 4, West Fannin Elementary School, Blue Ridge, GA
- Culver, Kari, Grade 4, John Muir Elementary School, Portage, WI
- Daigle, Spencer, Grade 2, Nottingham Country Elementary School, Katy, TX
- D'Alterio, John, Grade 5, Holy Child School, Old Westbury, NY
- Danaher, Colleen, Grade 6, Huntington Place Elementary School, Northport, AL
- Daniel, Cody, Grade 2, Iuka Elementary School, Iuka, MS
- Davies, Allison, Grade 5, Maple Ridge Elementary School, Somerset, PA
- DeGeeter, Matthew, Grade 2, Lincoln School, Morton, IL
- Dewald, Lindsey, Grade 4, Barcelona Hills School, Mission Viejo, CA
- Dittoe, Nicole, Grade 2, Villa Madonna Academy, Villa Hills, KY
- Drace, Kevin, Grade 7, Huntsville Middle School, Huntsville, AL
- Dubridge, Jenny, Grade 4, Valley View School, Rockford, MI
- Ecker, Christine, Grade 3, Joseph Azevada School, Fremont, CA
- Ehresman, Ryan, Grade 2, Ethel R. Jones School, Portage, IN
- Evans, David, Grade 4, Stewart Elementary School, Bradenton, FL
- Fletcher, Billy, Grade 3, Windsor School, Elyria, OH
- Fohl, Stephen, Grade 2, Fort Irwin Elementary School, Yermo, CA

•Franks, Jennifer, Grade 6, Huntington Place Elementary School, Northport, AL

•Fricano, Thomas, Grade 3, St. Finbar School, Brooklyn, NY

•Galan, Sandie, Grade 5, Russell Elementary School, Los Angeles, CA

•George, Gabriel, Grade 8, Richbourg Middle School, Crestview, FL

•Gilchrist, Kate, Grade 1, Carney Elementary School, Baltimore, MD

•Gill, Brooke, Grade 7, T.S. Hill Middle School, Dexter, MO

•Gonzalez, Monica, Grade 5, Friona Grade School, Friona, TX

•Griffith, Crystal Lynn, Grade 5, Dillingham Intermediate School, Sherman, TX

•Hall, Marques, Grade 5, Badillo Elementary School, Covina, CA

•Hallal, Nida, Kindergarten, St. Paschal Baylon School, Cleveland, OH

•Halliday, Lauren, Grade 6, Monroe County Middle School, Tompkinsville, KY

•Hamedih, Leila, Grade 3, Luiseno Elementary School, Corona, CA

•Harvey, Hollie, Grade 6, Boone Elementary School, Barbourville, KY

•Heathcock, Jonathan, Grade 5, William Gay, McAlester, OK

•Hecker, Amy, Grade 5, Roosevelt Elementary School, Dickinson, ND

•Heffern, Damien, Grade 9, Monroe Academy, Forsyth, GA

•Hilliard, Sean, Grade 8, Richbourg Middle School, Crestview, FL

•Huddy, Kaleigh, Grade 2, Fort Irwin Elementary School, Yermo, CA

•Hullinger, Rikki, Grade 7, Robert K. Shafer Middle School, Bensalem, PA

•Irvin, John Douglas III, Grade 1, Delta C-7 Schools, Deering, MO

•Johnson, Sarah, Grade 2, New Haven Elementary School, Union, KY

•Johnson, Stacey, Grade 2, North Shore School, Duluth, MN

•Judd, Meghann, Grade 3, Hughes-Elizabeth Lakes Union School, Lake Hughes, CA

•Katzman, Mike, Grade 7, Carrithers Middle School, Louisville, KY

•Kitchenmaster, Dale, Grade 2, Fairview School, Mora, MN

•Krakau, Derrick, Grade 5, Meadowview School, Oak Creek, WI

•Kurup, Aaron, Grade 3, Joseph Azevada School, Fremont, CA

•Lainson, Tyler, Grade 7, Kirn Junior High School, Council Bluffs, IA

•LaMonte, Marlo, Grade 1, West Hurley Elementary School, West Hurley, NY

•Lang, Matthew, Grade 4, Calvert Street School, Woodland Hills, CA

•LaPointe, Sarah, Grade 2, Hardwick Elementary School, Gilbertville, MA

•Larsen, Nik, Grade 6, Sacred Heart School, Ely, NV

•Lassus, Don, Grade 5, Kate Bell School, Houston, TX

•Law, Katy, Grade 6, Race Brook School, Orange, CT

•Lawler, Courtney, Grade 5, Hidden Forest Elementary School, San Antonio, TX

•Lindeman, Josh, Grade 4, Newport Elementary, Newport, MN

•Lopez, Lena, Grade 3, Annaville Elementary School, Corpus Christi, TX

•Lopez, Moniqa, Grade 4, Baker Elementary School, San Diego, CA

•Maertz, Danah, Grade 7, Alhambra Traditional School, Phoeniz, AZ

•Marlune, Allison, Kindergarten, St. Paschal Baylon School, Cleveland, OH

•McAllister, Mary, Grade 8, St. John the Baptist School, Green Bay, WI

•McKinley, Joei, Grade 5, Luther C. Barnes Elementary School, Owasso, OK

•McMurray, Justin, Grade 3, Coweta Central Elementary School, Coweta, OK

•Mehall, Heather, Kindergarten, Lincoln Elementary School, Stockton, CA

•Melchiori, Elisa, Grade 6, St. Brigid School, San Francisco, CA

•Mezzanotte, Tom, Grade 3, McKenna Elementary School, Massapequa Park, NY

•Miller, Aaron, Grade 4, Read Turrentine Elementary School, Silsbee, TX

•Mills, Emily, Grade 5, Cajon Park School, Santee, CA

•Mitulinski, Justin, Grade 6, St. Matthias, Youngstown, OH

•Morris, Matt, Grade 4, Holy Family Education Center, San Jose, CA

•Moseley, Misti, Grade 7, Ooltewah Middle School, Ooltewah, TN

- Naylor, Astria, Grade 4, Robertson Elementary School, Round Rock, TX
- Nekos, Peter, Grade 1, West Hurley Elementary School, West Hurley, NY
- Nelson, Rebecca, Grade 3, Collet Park Elementary School, Albuquerque, NM
- O'Brien, Elizabeth, Grade 7, Robert K. Shafer Middle School, Bensalem, PA
- O'Donnell, Kaitlin, Grade 4, Jackson School, Newton, MA
- Omlor, Timothy, Grade 1, Kralltown Elementary School, East Berlin, PA
- Owens, Thomas, Grade 6, Marengo Academy, Linden, AL
- Passeri, Christy, Grade 1, Roosevelt School, Eynon, PA
- Peterson, Tiffany, Grade 4, Luiseno Elementary School, Corona, CA
- Petruzzi, Lori Beth, Grade 5, Fleetwood School, Mt. Laurel, NJ
- Phillips, Stacy, Grade 3, Dupont Elementary School, Dupont, IN
- Phillips, Veronica, Grade 5, Margaret Bell Miller School, Waynesburg, PA
- Piatt, Katy, Grade 6, Chewning Middle School, Durham, NC
- Pierce, Amber, Grade 8, Charity Middle School, Rose Hill, NC
- Plaisance, Collette, Grade 2, Fairview School, Mora, MN
- Quader, Arshia, Grade 8, Troy Junior High School, Troy, OH
- Ramsower, Mary, Grade 4, Timberwilde Elementary School, San Antonio, TX
- Ritz, Anthony, Grade 3, Harris Elementary School, Collingdale, PA
- Roberts, Samantha, Grade 3, Anderson Elementary School, Anderson, MO
- Rosenfeld, Kate, Grade 3, Scott School, Warwick, RI
- Rountree, Lucas, Grade 4, Carmichael Elementary, Houston, TX
- Rowleau, John, Grade 3, Twinbrook Elementary School, Rockville, MD
- Samaan, Miray, Grade 6, Brockton Christian School, Brockton, MA
- Sandherr, Sarah, Grade 7, Lackawanna Trail High School, Factoryville, PA
- Sanieoff, Erica, Grade 4, Solomon Schechter Day School, Newton Center, MA
- Schulman, Christopher, Grade 6, Piedmont Middle School, San Jose, CA
- Short, Alia, Grade 3, Frankford Township School, Branchville, NJ
- Simek, Stacy, Grade 5, Fleetwood School, Mt. Laurel, NJ
- Simmons, Laurie, Grade 6, Renner Middle School, Plano, TX
- Smith, Contessa, Grade 3, Purvis Attendance Center, Purvis, MS
- Sparks, Jeff, Grade 6, Brunswick R-II School, Brunswick, MO
- Spell, Kristin, Grade 6, Sampson Middle School, Clinton, NC
- Stickell, Kathryn, Grade 7, Benton Middle School, Benton, LA
- Stork, Rachel, Grade 4, Fairview School, Carroll, IA
- Sugimoto, Mandy, Grade 4, Davis Elementary School, Austin, TX
- Sunshine, Michael, Grade 4, Luiseno Elementary School, Corona, CA
- Sutton, Michael A., Grade 5, St. Anthony, San Antonio, FL
- Tapazian, Mark, Grade 8, Hannah Middle School, East Lansing, MI
- Torres, Belen, Grade 5, Friona Grade School, Friona, TX
- Unruh, Kamielle, Grade 5, Wheatland Elementary School, Valley Center, KS
- Vallejo, Nicole, Grade 8, Edwards School, Chicago, IL
- Van Lanen, Caroline, Grade 2, Lindbergh School, Madison, WI
- Venegas, Vincent, Grade 4, Mitchell Elementary School, Racine, WI
- Vincent, Aaron, Grade 2, Vera Wilsie Elementary School, Newaygo, MI
- Watson, Susan, Grade 2, Vogel Elementary School, Wrentham, MA
- Watts, Stephanie, Grade 8, St. Paul's, Danville, IL
- Weber, Brooke, Grade 3, Clover Hill Elementary School, Midlothian, VA
- Weeks, Jillian, Grade 6, McKenna Elementary School, Massapequa Park, NY
- Werger, Christopher, Grade 5, Central Elementary School, Allison Park, PA
- Willis, Amy, Grade 5, Mt. Vernon Elementary School, Lemon Grove, CA
- Zeller, Lisa, Grade 8, Paxico Junior High School, Paxico, KS